Read and Play
Giant Machines

by Jim Pipe

Stargazer Books
Mankato, Minnesota

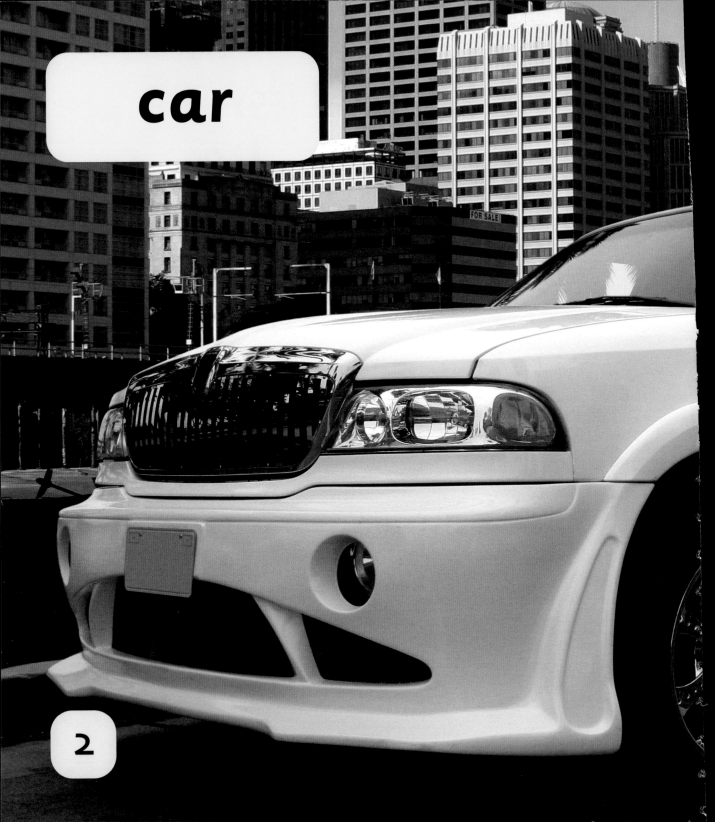

car

This giant **car** is very big!

3

truck

A giant **truck** is very heavy.

4

5

robot

This giant **robot** is scary!

helicopter

This **helicopter** is very strong.

8

submarine

This **submarine** is very long.

plane

This **plane** is very wide.

rocket

A **rocket** is very tall.

digger

This giant **digger** works fast.

17

ship

This giant **ship** is long and wide.

What am I?

train

wheel

ship

tank

Match the words and pictures.

How many?

Can you count the big ships?

21

What noise?

Crunch!

Chucka!

Whoosh!

Roar!

 22 Can you sound like these machines?

Index

For Parents and Teachers

Questions you could ask:

p. 2 How many people can fit in this car? This Chrysler 300 is over 16 feet (5 meters) long and nearly 7 feet (2 meters) wide. It can fit up to 16 passengers.

p. 4 Can you see the ladder? The truck is so big the driver needs a ladder to climb up into the cab. The truck works at a mine carrying heavy rocks.

p. 6 What does the giant robot look like? The 40-foot (12-meter)-tall robot is built like a dragon (it breathes fire) and can crush a car in its claws.

p. 8 What is the helicopter doing? Point out the heavy load slung in a net below the helicopter (a Chinook). It is carrying food and other supplies to people during a disaster.

p. 10 What can a submarine do? A submarine can travel underwater (for weeks at a time). Point out the crew on the deck to show the size of the vessel.

p. 12 Look at all the windows! This Airbus 380 can carry up to 555 passengers. It can fly over 9,000 miles (15,000 kilometers) without stopping.

p. 14 What is carrying the rocket? A huge truck (the biggest in the world) carries the rocket to the launch pad. The man and van give a sense of scale.

p. 18 Can you see the swimming pool? This ship, the Seven Seas Voyager, is a floating hotel. Ships like this are the biggest machines in the world.

Activities you could do:

• Ask readers to describe or draw the biggest machine they have seen: comparing its size to other objects, how many people it carries, what it does etc.

• Go outside and ask readers to measure out how big the machines are, e.g. if one pace is 18 inches (roughly 0.5 m) long, the giant car on pages 2-3 is about 10 paces long. The ship on pages 18-19 is over 400 paces long (650 feet or 200 meters).

• Role play: ask the reader to imagine driving a giant machine, e.g. climbing up into a truck's cab, sailing in a submarine or flying a jumbo jet.

© Aladdin Books Ltd 2009

Designed and produced by
Aladdin Books Ltd

First published in 2009 in the United States by
Stargazer Books,
distributed by
Black Rabbit Books
PO Box 3263
Mankato, MN 56002

Library of Congress Cataloging-in-Publication Data
Pipe, Jim, 1966-
  Giant machines / Jim Pipe.
    p. cm. -- (Read and play)
  Includes bibliographical references and index.
  Summary: "In very simple language and photographs, describes large vehicles such as rockets and submarines. Includes quizzes and games"--Provided by publisher.
  ISBN 978-1-59604-178-3
  1. Motor vehicles--Sizes--Juvenile literature. 2. Ships--Juvenile literature. I. Title.
  TL147.P573 2009
  428.1--dc22
                                2008015284

Series consultant
Zoe Stillwell is an experienced preschool teacher.

Photocredits:
l-left, r-right, b-bottom, t-top, c-center, m-middle
All photos from istockphoto.com except: 2-3, 6-7, 10-11, 20br, 22br, 23bl & bmr—US Navy. 4-5, 23br—Vladimir Lukovic/Dreamstime.com. 8-9, 22tr, 23ml—US Army. 14, 23tr—NASA. 15—Corbis. 18-19, 23tmr—courtesy Regent Seven Seas cruises.